1996

SARA PETERS

ANANSI

Published in 2013 by House of Anansi Press Inc.
110 Spadina Avenue, Suite 801, Toronto, Ontario, M5V 2K4
Tel. 416-363-4343 · Fax 416-363-1017 · www.houseofanansi.com

Distributed in Canada by HarperCollins Canada Ltd.
1995 Markham Road, Scarborough, M1B 5M8
Toll free tel. 1-800-387-0117

Distributed in the USA by Publishers Group West
1700 Fourth Street, Berkley, California 94710
Toll free tel. 1-800-788-3123

House of Anansi Press is committed to protecting our natural environment.
As part of our efforts, the interior of this book is printed on paper made from
second-growth forests and is acid-free.

Library and Archives Canada Cataloguing in Publication

Peters, Sara, 1982-
1996 / Sara Peters.
Issued also in electronic format.
ISBN 978-1-77089-271-2 (pbk).—ISBN 978-1-77089-348-1 (bound.)
I. Title.
PS8631.E824O64 2013   C811'.6   C2012-906718-0

Library of Congress Control Number:
2012950664

Cover & text design: Brian Morgan
Typesetting: Lynn Gammie

17 16 15 14 13   1 2 3 4 5

Printed and bound in Canada

We acknowledge for their financial support of our publishing program
the Canada Council for the Arts, the Ontario Arts Council, and the
Government of Canada through the Canada Book Fund.

For my family and friends

IV

I HATED IT; I EXPECT EVERYONE SECRETLY DID

V

YOU LOVE THIS ORPHAN, MANY PEOPLE DO

VI

I AM WALKING THROUGH WATER

I

IN MY DREAMS I AM A MORAL CHILD

BABYSITTERS

Your mother was as nubile as a dressmaker's dummy;
your father polished his glasses and rubbed his crop.
When the Babysitter arrived, with her turquoise belt
and raw mouth, your father had never seen
such a fine wrist, such a way with an onion!
She pinned a plastic hummingbird
behind one pink ear; she sang "Fever"
over boiling eggs.
You, at nine,
sculpted your curls with toothpaste. You hated
your friends: their Lego sets and down jackets.
But this Babysitter. She'd start with Goldilocks, then
veer. Papa Bear said *Someone has been eating my porridge!*
And Goldilocks said *My life is broken, my heart is over.*
Snap my neck like a broccoli stalk.
Hear the Babysitter: brisk and newsy to the milkman.
You catch words like *cream, coffee, cows*; phrases like
my sister in Florida, 8 pounds 10 ounces,
a head of black down! But when she thinks herself
alone, you hear *back seat of the car,* then
with a trench knife, in the orchard. Secrets thud
like June bugs against screens,
and all you have to do is let them in.

PLAYING LESBIANS

for Jessica

In my dreams I am a moral child,
And once I tire of performing

My idiosyncrasies, my babysitter and I
Are somewhere still sinking

Into a dimpled couch, under a misremembered painting,
Playing lesbians. There was what I was and then

There was what I seemed to be becoming:
I love this gory business, I kept thinking,

As I watched (with the eye that wasn't
Pressed into the couch) the wind shunt one of her hairs

Over the hardwood floor, and heard
A sudden rain begin, silvery and short—barely enough

To wet an umbrella. Some omissions are so extravagant
They become adornment. With August over

And linden trees no longer
Buzzing emporiums, in front of my parents she licked

An eyelash off my cheek: for scrapbooking, for luck.
And we all made sounds that groped toward laughter.

I watched her pull on her scalloped shoes,
Each heel so high her steps like needlepoint,

Bright dust beneath each brow's cathedral arch,
My face swept for a second by one of her thousands

Of polished rococo ringlets, as—for and since it was my birthday—
She fastened gold chains to my ankles and wrists.

CRUELTY

When I was eleven, I watched my cousin cut open a gopher
with the serrated top of a tin can.

I see this cousin now: straight shoulders, straight hair.
Each eye bright and sharp as a rhinestone.

She knows a thing will yield if spoken to gently,
so she doesn't waste time on incense

and Sarah Vaughan. Last night, three girls at a bus stop
beat an old man to death with black umbrellas. And here I am

bound to elaborate on the state of his glasses,
knocked off his head and spinning into air

that shimmered with rain. Yet everyone, when small,
has come in from the river with something half-dead

in the bottom of a bucket, and no one expects that to become
their defining moment. Now I want to find a red door

and live behind it. I want to talk taxes and fiscal responsibility.
But her under voice is sleepless as a shark.

It says *break that window. Dial that number.*
At eleven, it pulled me from the TV, and led me

up the driveway, behind a parked Subaru, to a square
of dead November grass. The wind was fresh

and sweet as an apple, as she brought the metal down
with a calm hand, teeth denting her lower lip.

And she steadied the animal, saying
shhh, stay still, don't worry, my dad's a vet.

WINTER JEWELRY

She was thirty-four,
    she'd recently chopped off her right index finger

and she came to my high school for recess and lunch.
    I felt her before I saw her:

she ran her hand down my spine
    It happened so fast I had no time to pose.

Nothing felt better to me
    than being touched possessively,

without having to touch someone back.
    She'd pull my braid, pick lint off my sweater,

smooth my eyebrows, all while explaining
    saffron and fisting and France.

Once, she tightened my scarf
    and we drove to her rented cabin, until the road stopped

and we were walking through snow
    falling at inaudible frequencies.

She sang something under her breath
    (she said it was nothing I knew),

striding ahead in unlaced boots, her jacket flapping open.
    She wore so many layers, I'd never been able to tell

the actual size of her body, beyond the occasional ankle or wrist
   breaking the surface. Around her the stars spun like tops:

tops I knew she could pause with her fingertip.
   When we arrived,

she lit twenty tea lights and vanished.
   Then animals began to emerge.

Two patchy dogs from the couch,
   while in one corner, something nursed on something else.

There was a mirror
   the size of a record jacket, and in it I saw her

walking out of the bathroom toward me,
   her bandage half unrolled: the wound was startling.

I opened my beer and watched
   as the foam ran down my hand and wrist

and she flew—it seemed—to my side,
   knelt, took the bottle, and said

Put your mouth on it
   and when I bent she laughed

as a cat dropped down near her knee,
   from what seemed a great height, though it couldn't be.

POSTFEMINISM

From the beginning
you should know I'm embellishing,
but was I ever twelve?

Swan Lake,
disco-ball lamps,
the walls cracker-thin,

Emily first up?
What happened
when her mother stepped outside

to flap the plastic tablecloth?
Only what we later embellished.
Her mother's broken-armed boyfriend

helped us sift
through the jewelry box:
a mermaid pendant

with eyes of lapis lazuli;
the drugstore opals.
The letter M was shaved into the back

of Emily's head—
that's the side of me, she said,
that no one knows.

The boyfriend's broken arm
unslung nightly from its cloth.
I slept over once a month, at twelve—

we glued magazine pages
to the bedroom door: *Cheapr Medz*
For A Longr, Thickr.

She'll Blow Her Mind
When She Gets A Load.
We shaved our eyebrows

and danced in the living room
wearing the boyfriend's plaid shirts,
Emily's mother

waiting patiently on the porch,
snapping compacts
like finger cymbals,

or painting her toenails salmon.
When the boyfriend rolled his arm
back into the sling, off for the evening,

we did that usual thing:
ran water hotter
than we could stand.

II
TWO DAYS BEFORE THE WEDDING

MARY ELLEN SPOOK

for Marjorie

In the early twentieth century, a farming couple living outside
of Antigonish, Nova Scotia, adopted a young woman named
Mary Ellen. In 1922, strange things began to happen.

As a teenager, there are several ways to get your parents' attention.
  Only one of these ways is to set things on fire with your mind.

But Mary Ellen was unaware of the alternatives.
  Had it not been 1922, had she been born yesterday,

she could've banged out a career, like Sylvia Browne.
  Book jackets bright as tinfoil, rosy quartz,

incantatory moaning set to djembes.
  Had it not been Nova Scotia, she could've joined a circus,

called herself Isis, read hibiscus, cut a fringe,
  fucked a few dogs when the seekers slowed their seeking.

But what she lacked was access.
  No books, no newspaper even—

the closest thing to freakish the Francophone farmhand
  with his black cigarettes and black coffee.

She didn't *mean* to braid the horses' manes and tails
  hundreds of times with so much élan—French, four-stranded—

but up was the only unoccupied direction,
  so how else to get there? And always

these questions: *Who set those fires?*
    Who broke those mirrors? Is that your blood?

One morning, the china cabinet doors
    flew open of their own accord,

and teacups floated out in a straight line,
    doing a little turn at the end of their journey, like runway models.

This time, Mary Ellen hadn't even been there
    throwing her big wet mind around. Instead,

she'd been standing at the edge of the property,
    where the plough always turned back. Her neck was bent

like a medieval mandolin.
    When the priests and parents approached—

already bloody, from pushing
    through blackberry thorns—

their faces were no longer
    the human faces she had known.

So she lay down before them
    carefully, as if upon dozens of glass balls,

and when someone made the first cut, she said only
    Mother, I am afraid.

WRONGHEADED

In Fatima, Portugal, in 1917, the Virgin Mary reportedly appeared to three local shepherd children—one of the children was named Jacinta.

The Virgin Mary first appeared in April, floating, dressed in white
(of course), with beautiful bare feet, pointing to a disembodied yet

Immaculate Heart a little to the right above a half-grown pine.
Jacinta shut her eyes and tucked her lips behind her teeth. When asked

later what language the Virgin spoke, she said
it was not Portuguese

and none she had heard, but rather like poured light
gradually resolving into words.

Jacinta was nine during that first apparition.
Thereafter, she developed a system.

She fed her lunch to the sheep and ate handfuls of chokecherries
that sucked all the moisture from her cheeks.

During days of weakness,
she'd wrap her knees in cloth before beginning the morning

trek to the shrine, where she knelt for hours
before Our Lady revealed Herself. But after being shown

the wounds this opened in Our Lord's palms,
Jacinta discarded the cloth.

Only a few pebbles worked their way into her kneecap.
(Jacinta had a sweet voice and loved dancing.)

Poor Virgin Mary! I am very sad for sinners. This sadness alleviated a bit
by rhythmic scratching of the skin on her wrists. The way to the shrine

was harder in summer: distractions of violets, warm buzz of wind.
Thirsty, eyes running

farther back in her head than anyone could see,
Jacinta knew her way to Heaven

would be thorned, yet negotiable, though many rosaries were needed
to haul her dead relations up from Purgatory—

rosaries like the rope she knotted around her waist.
All children are orphans not knowing the pain of Our Lord.

One morning, the Virgin said *Collect the country people
and Our Lord will perform a miracle.* When later in the day

a crowd of thirty thousand assembled, the sun
spun like a bicycle wheel, then plunged toward the thirty thousand
    faces.

The newspapermen shrieked, a Priest shut his eyes and smiled and
    swayed a little.
Jacinta also shut her eyes, fearing an occasion of sin:

her proof, her pride, her pleasure in
the flung sun's heat on the part in her hair.

CRYPTID

You saw her once, at Margaree Harbour,
when you were a three-year-old boy called Oscar.

While you staggered over the sand,
slippery with SPF 50,

your parents humped on the beach towel,
to Lou Reed singing "Sweet Jane."

Lipless, lidless, five slits in her throat,
her rosy larynx furled in and out.

You laughed at her boa: seaweed, rusted forks.
She tore up a starfish, swallowed its points.

You offered, as truce, some Sun-Maid raisins.
She spread out, to amuse you, all forty fingers.

Finding you gone, your father sprinted over the sand
(long-legged, in one Birkenstock)

while your mother stayed *right there!*, sat on her heels,
gasping into a brown paper bag.

Later, your parents noticed the salt taste of your skin,
called you their potato chip.

Your mother combed sand from your hair,
your father found beach grass in your bed.

Now they sleep to the sound of rogue waves crashing. Dreaming,
they pick their way through dying jellyfish

to find you waiting (not for them) behind a rock,
content amid the iridescent quivering.

NORWAY HOUSE, 1982

I.

This person the nuns call Mother—eighteen and pregnant—
    comes to the abbey for Family Hour:
        plastic bags of milk, gingerbread at noon—

but when the nuns say
    we have a tool shed, full bath and futon,
        this Mother does not hesitate:

the town is tiny and she has few friends.
    Now she rises when the nuns do, cooks and mops,
        embroiders leather mitts, and does not pray.

These nuns at first
    seem identical in their habits—slow chewing, exquisite
        concentration—later she sees them revealed

by their hands, each pair more bare
    than the face. When she wakes up
        to a set of these hands on her cheeks, the nun leaning over her says

come down to the lake. The night is not over. Walking toward water
    nuns loosen and drift. She thinks
        she hears giggling pass between some; she later decides

she was wrong. They pause under pine trees;
    one nun empties her shoe. The Mother lets
        a mantis step off a branch and onto her neck: its body made
            almost entirely

out of its footless legs, and she imagines her shiver
    as a neon helix coiling down through water
        —hastening that unwanted heartbeat.

2.

Having apparently tried to reach water
    after being shot in the chest,
        having instead collapsed on the sand, this bear:

each eye dehydrating slowly, fur alive with lice,
    whole body thrown violently forward
        as if against a rein, as if about to reach

the outer limits of a dream.
    One nun begins to hum.
        Nearby, some kids are coming through the brush,

carrying paper sacks from the corner store.
    They start with shells and kelp, then move to candy
        as they decorate the bear like a cake. One frames the wound

with licorice whips; one trims the spine with red gumdrops.
    The nuns say *we are lucky*
        they didn't come with knives and hammers.

When the nuns touch the bear
    they pull their sleeves down
        over their clean, muscular hands

so it's not really touching at all. The Mother studies her mitt:
    the hibiscus flower, worked in pink beads,
        that roots at her wrist

and blooms on her palm, till
one nun removes it,
and forces the Mother's bare hand to the animal's head.

MAY

Two days before the wedding
The fields whiten with circus tents

Some of us are sent to the barn
To tear apart chickens
Chatting and stacking

Their livers and hearts
Others collect stray children

And run them in circles
Till they're exhausted
When the bride paces

We nestle her into corners
Work ointment into her hands

One day before the wedding
She tracks us to the river
Since it is May

The water's silvered with gaspereau
And she watches as we sieve them up

To spasm on the dock
Gulping splintered air
Rubbing off their spangled skins

III
EVERYONE'S A SERIOUS SEVENTEEN

RED CLOTH

I went to this party, I stared at a man in orange glasses,
And then there was nothing to do
Except follow his red cloth shoes to the beach.

I buried the base of my glass and watched
As (naked) he staggered too close to the waves—

I sat in the sand and counted my bracelets.
The man in orange glasses said
Cape Breton's so green—like living inside a salad!

Then he fell backwards
Trying to trace a castle in the stars.

I am not sure why I'm convinced
That expressing contempt is my life's work—
And I should've been back at that party

Building my own complex salad,
Using unimpeachably local mushrooms (grown

On my body), not here, watching these waves
Throw the same length of chain at the shore.
And why do I crave not the shaved

And lotioned surface of his or any
Body, but only the tangy,

Throbbing interior? Wet wheels spinning, wet looms weaving,
One red tissue after another
Torn by my reach?

ROMANCE

Everyone's a serious seventeen.
And so, one night, we married in the woods—
though having to make curfew spoiled the mood.

You wore, of course, a kind of smock.
I was bright as a jester in metres
of daffodil gauze, my metals

dyeing my skin. We had, we knew, it all:
the chalices, the incense, the Lovers' Tarot deck—
and, nearby, the baptizing rush of river. *The air smells*

like the mulch of primeval concupiscence! I cried,
and what could you do but agree?
Ants traveled patiently under our raiment;

the sex was athletic and wise…
and then we touched foreheads
with a new strain of sorrowful dignity,

for although we were rural,
we were never deep enough in to mistake
the humming of wires overhead.

THE SWORD DANCE

for Michelle

There were so many things I hated, at seven:
group activities, talking, children
    younger than me,

and how Meghan, my dance teacher,
loved the other kid, despite
    his sloppiness:

drooling, tripping, kicking the metre sticks
we crossed in an X
    to practice the Sword Dance—

(which used to be done only after the enemy died)—

and I watched Meghan's throat spend the whole hour heating
the metal necklace she wore.
    I smiled as hard as I had been taught,

though I couldn't stand seeing
her satiny arms around that dirty eater,
    his nose so close

to the strawberry birthmark on her cheek
that she touched whether happy or sad.
    Each night I lay in bed

punching my stomach, hoping this practice might make it

so that next time, Meghan and I
would be alone. But every week
     there he was,

rat-tailed and panting,
and every week I tied
     my black leather laces so tight up my calves

the X's remain.
I wanted to jump so high that I'd spend
     an hour at least only falling,

and hit every planet on my way to the concrete floor.

I wanted to see him walked
up the basement stairs,
     through the warm,

plaid-papered kitchen,
given an apple
     and maybe

his shoes,
coaxed through
     the sliding glass doors to the porch,

then dragged to the woodshed and strangled.

MY SOUL AND I, WE WERE SENSITIVE

My soul and I, we were sensitive,
And our project was to process
Unrequited love—
So we pitched a tent near the ocean, at night,
In a field of chilled violets and lavender.
My soul nicknamed me Radical Embodiment.
Together, we scrambled down cliffs to the inlet,
Grabbing the same
Handfuls of poison oak,
Then we'd wade into the water,
Smoking, and later
We built a fire,
And did pagan twirls around it.
Doing this, I cringed,
Yet my soul pretended
Violent indifference, just
Folding its useless wings lest they be singed.

I UNDERSTOOD OUR TIME WAS RUNNING OUT

for Julie

I understood our time was running out,
so I planned a winter picnic, and privately decided
not to eat. We drove past petrified trees,
and thankfully we passed a cyclist
with prayer cards woven through his spokes—
so he provided talk until
we reached the cove. You spread a collapsed cardboard box
over sea grass blown the wrong way,
while I unpacked my obvious fruits and vegetables:
pomegranate, artichoke heart, cherry.
Some people bag the first head they see.
I'd chosen lettuce as carefully
as a ball gown, comparing ruffles.
But soon we were noting a summer A-frame,
nodding our emptying heads, and as if at a chess game
we stared at the square foot between us.
Soon I'd try on your glasses, you'd play with my lighter,
a few feet away foam came off the water
and dolloped the rocks, and a plastic doll torso
was eight waves away from arriving:
armless legless sucked and beaten clean.

IV
I HATED IT; I EXPECT EVERYONE SECRETLY DID

HAIR

In this second of terror the child
sees herself as hair and sees her hair
as it is seen: unwashed for one year,
unbrushed for two, and now her scalp itches
to the tangled roots of each eye.
She knows her every bone
has been whittled to an arrow that points to her hair,
and every eye she meets becomes
a butcher's hook from which she hangs.
What would the dresser find, if he cut in?
A doorless house—a table set for none.

MORDECHAI

His name is Mordechai.
His hair will be cut next month.
Sometimes I see him

driving down Laurier
in his sturdy plastic car, his mother
jogging lightly beside him in her heavy shoes.
He says
Who are you?
to each passerby.
It seems he's memorized

the particular slap
of my roommate Ben's sneakers
on the fourteen iron steps that separate his floor from ours.

He's been cleaning his plastic car all morning,
using old long johns
and water that spills from the drainpipe under the awning.
When Ben jackhammers down the stairs—
his pink ears almost transparent in the sun—

Mordechai's waiting
with his mother standing behind him,

her hands covering his shoulders and part of his chest.
Her black hat hides her brows
and the luminous square of her forehead.
Good morning, she says, *my son has a question.*

And Ben says
Cool car someday let me drive it
and to the mother *Sorry I'm just so late,*
maybe tonight?

The mother unbuttons
then rebuttons her cuffs, and Mordechai

watches Ben's red hair to the end of the block.
Then he turns

and tucks himself behind the wheel,
like Ophelia he floats down the street in his plastic car.

CAMDEN 14

One November morning he woke up
    and a new white world had slid into place.

He'd been kept awake all night

by snowflakes, so Camden
    set himself on fire.

No, try something like:

he caulked for hours to seal his doors and windows,
    but everyone kept getting in:

the landlady, who said he was so polite, for a boy of fourteen,

and not *just* because he never spoke;
    the one-house-over girl, insane at eight because made to wait

every winter morning on her lawn,

turning pink then blue then in circles,
    or his mother standing

in a triangle of sunlight, wrapping

the phone cord around her wrists,
    whispering down the black plastic something about

his sister: they'd found her in the park,

found her, drugged her, roped her ankles
and pulled her over the grass, like a canoe.

It was Thursday, Camden lived above a corner store,

and the cashier saw him first
(her red hair streaked with purple, like ribbon candy.)

He poured the gasoline, he lit a match, the match his pole,

his vault so clean,
the white world dropped away.

"DEAD BOY HAD TOO MANY INJURIES TO FIT IN ONE DRAWING"

Jérémy on his birthday morning,
   in his own ballooned house,
      with a party going on,

         hiding behind the recycling bin,
            because he stepped on a Lego
            and shrieked. His father says Jérémy wants

to look like his mother,
     with gold fawns (like hers)
        in his ears—

         and it's true that he loves
           how his mother stands up
           and pulls the comb from her hair

when his father walks through the door. Outside,
   five party children hide from a sixth,
      who lies face down on a mattress,

         counting, while an interview spills
           from the stereo. What used to happen to him
           only at night now also happens

during the day, so his parents dress him
    incongruously: long sleeves and layers in August.
        He watches as his mother sets on the table

            a violet-stuffed jam jar,
                and his father takes off the stove
                    an oil-spitting frying pan, and asks

if Jérémy wants some man
    to bring him flowers like that, one day.
        Outside, party children one by one

            put thumbs in their mouths,
                and turn to the house, listening—
                    then Jérémy's mother

bangs through the screen door and screams

HEYHEYHEYLOOK

sliding the stereo volume up to max,
    dancing baroquely and alone
        to the weather report,

            letting each bra strap
                fall off its shoulder,
                    while in her ears the gold fawns jerk and shudder.

ABORTION

I hated it; I expect everyone secretly did.

I hadn't yet seen blood besides my own,
and then only from a knee or finger.

Posters were distributed according to age:
I was six, and so given the six-week photo.
The adults got second

or third trimester blowups.
We split up, to catch the cars both ways.
One poster featured a twenty-two-week fetus, its head held
by latexed fingers, an American quarter

sitting in the surrounding blood,
flipped to the side that said
In God We Trust. Sometimes we'd share the highway
with craftspeople selling wooden elves, or woolly welcome mats,
or tiny tin houses glued with dried flowers and fruit.

The gravel shoulder was bright with trash,
and drivers sometimes spat or tossed takeout,
but it was only twice a year, this protest of
The New Holocaust, as my poster proclaimed,
and soon enough I could be back
with my five clean dolls, in my hexagram room.

V
YOU LOVE THIS ORPHAN, MANY PEOPLE DO

MY SISTER AND I, WE KNOW WE ARE FILTH

My sister and I, we know we are filth, and so we proceed with great caution
    when we enter the world that was saved for us—

      unlocking our mother's door, prying open her chest,
      plunging our hands in the powder and silk—

we know we could be in her bedroom for years,
    and yet we forgot to pack meat for our journey.

      Orchids and lilies pattern her walls. When we tire of smelling
    our own bodies, we spray her perfume in the air

and it rises in a sparkling fount, lingers, then falls. Now
    I rip a velvet headband with my teeth. I spit

      the sequins at my sister. Now she is using our mother's tweezers
    to pluck black hairs from beneath her navel,

while I turn my face to the vaulted ceiling
    and hold my breath till the sparks come.

      We know we are in this, up to our waists. But still we're ashamed
    to want what we cannot name. My sister's trailing her tongue

across our mother's mirror, and I am imagining this unnameable something
    passing swiftly out of her, as I want it passing swiftly out of me—

      but we both know the dark will come on
    like someone pushing their thumbs into our eyes—

our mother will find us here and stride toward us
arms and coat open to show she means no harm—

CLIPS FROM BEOWULF'S ADOLESCENCE

I.

Better find him a local
Before he ruins another sheep.
No older than eight, no darker than honey, hair curly,
Scrub her with salt.

2.

Bagpipes or drums?
Water or rocks?
The pit or the cave?
Eight dogs or twelve?

3.

He should not have carved
His name on her back.
He should not have twisted her neck
So profoundly.

4.

(Rehooked her earrings.
Retrieved each freckled leg.
The cliffs around them
Crumbling, chalky, pink streaked.)

SPRING RITES

It's April in Halifax and the homeless people are coming out
    to Chisholm's annual lobster boil.
At the end of his street,

half on the sidewalk,
    is a woman rolled in a camouflage sleeping bag,
as if camped out for tickets. Chisholm sits outside

on an antique couch covered in gold brocade.
    The wires that run through his chest
emerge from his left ear,

and hook neatly over its rim.
    Yesterday he began
tearing the plastic sheets off his windows,

fluffing up his dirt lawn with a pitchfork,
    and buying lobsters
in preparation for the first of April.

He gets them cheaper from Peggys Cove,
    where planes routinely splat
into the Atlantic, and the lobsters caught have human hair

wrapped around their claws.
    He drags a cauldron from his basement
as people begin to arrive:

some who are normally found
       at intersections, reading sheet music,
some dangling dozens of tin pots

tied to their arms and legs,
       some wearing expertly slit garbage bags.
Chisholm's built a pyramid

of paper and branches,
       and soon the cauldron
puts out white blossoms of steam.

One man approaches in hip waders
       and sticks a finger through the lobsters' cage.
He speaks to the lobsters tenderly and at length,

and though they are bound
       they scramble faster against each other's backs
as if they can feel the humidity in the air,

as if they know what it means.
       Later, Chisholm sits back
and plays the accordion as the lobsters boil.

He will sieve them out when red,
       he will hand out silver tools,
he will struggle, discreetly, to dump out the seawater.

After eating, as in every year,
       the people make their nighttime preparations.
They stretch bungee cords between trees,

and over the cords they drape blankets,
    like children's tents.
They will sleep with fingers still green from tomalley.

Some have dogs that curl around their heads.
    One is on a bed of invisible daffodils
pushing every second through the soil.

Chisholm's gone to shower off
    more of his skin and hair. Now he's entered his bedroom,
pulled on socks and mitts, plugged himself back in—

and so eventually his daughter
    is the only one awake.
She weaves among the toppled bodies,

flying a ladybug kite.
    She's trying to avoid
the snapped-off feelers and the emptied claws.

BIONIC

My brother's twenty-two and therefore believes he's bionic.
He's home from school,
he's supposed to look after our mother for the week.
She's senile and probably dying.
He's cruel but his cruelty's probably temporary.

He's dressed her in a T-shirt that says
I kill everything I fuck // I fuck everything I kill.
She stares into a bowl of cornflake milk;
I carefully cover my breakfast in ketchup.

My brother is funny and blunt.
Whenever I say something sentimental,
or talk—for example—about the ocean,
he says, You know what?
You should write a *poem* about that.

(Right now I imagine we're all feeling
like it's winter and we're alone
in a splintering cabin on a crumbling cliff
with the ocean below hurling itself at the rocks
like a child against a locked bedroom door,
but of course I don't say this out loud.)

It's early spring; too cold to open windows.
We do it anyway. The air is ice and mud.
When we shiver our mother
lifts her head and says, I'll warm you up.
It's the first time she's talked in three days.
She says that as a child

she walked through a meadow for hours, following the smell of
    smoke—
parting tall grass as someone
might part a beaded curtain—until she found
an empty house
burning unattended in the dark.

YOUR LIFE AS LUCY MAUD MONTGOMERY

for Anastasia

*As a rule, I am very careful to be shallow and conventional where
depth and originality are wasted.*
- L.M.M., 1913

You love this orphan, many people do,
but your love's more advanced.
You wrap her in silk like a fly, weave wet,
bristling flowers into her hair, you asshole,
you love this orphan and around her you breathe
as if on a mountaintop, the sun in the process
of bending a rainbow behind your head.

You love this orphan, you lie in bed
rubbing your dry feet together,
thinking of the way she comes to you
requesting puffed sleeves, scholarship money,
you'd write off World War One for her, you *would*, except

she has you noting in this silly journal—
indigo tassel, pagoda watermark—
that she wants to marry a left-handed Aries
and be dropping babies by next week.
Soon she'll snip each braid and store it under glass,
she'll rope off her bedroom and charge
twenty-five at least for a look at her eyelet
pillowcases; you love this orphan,

you dickhead, but she's carrying a butterfly knife, although
you agreed last week to keep the gables green.
You love this orphan, many people do,

but your love's not advancing,
and she follows you to restaurants
looking tame as a doily in her pinafore,
but she stuffs your mouth with Styrofoam peanuts,
and places her knife on the thinnest skin you own.

VI
I AM WALKING THROUGH WATER

REHEARSAL

I am walking through water with one of my sisters,
    the river banked with tiger lilies, the sun
like having a lemon juiced into your eye, our senile dog

ecstatic behind us,
    and I am yammering
about my discovery—

a chest-deep pool, sentried by trees
    that caterpillars were killing
with their yearly carnival tents.

We reach then ruin the pool with oils and shampoos.
    We scrub too much skin
from our heels, then debate

whether to sunbathe naked:
    that is, who is hiding in the woods.
We joke so long and rough

the joke morphs, till we're practising for
    our future rapes:
we both have numbers that we know are up.

My sister's ears are speared
    with porcupine quills and steel,
but she's placed her straw hat carefully over her stomach.

As she talks I watch
        while dragonflies and other
less showy insects land

on her burning shoulders.
        The dragonflies present their stencilled wings.
I can't remember what the others do.

My sister spits
        to clean each sunglass mirror.
She wants me to hear

how, when it happens,
        she'll do this scream—
but when the scream comes it's just like she's opened

a shaken bottle of sparkling water:
        I am speechless only for the view
of her throat's cushioned corridor.

But when the scream ends her eyes
        have broken off from the rest of her face.
She takes our green net bag full of oranges

and slams it down on the baking rocks,
        beating the ground till the oranges soften
and streak the air with the smell of their breaking.

IN JUNE

Next door woman walks her son each morning
She is emptying their house
Placing every morning on the curb
Knobless drawers and lidless pots
She wears eight sapphire rings   an otter stole
Her son tucks dandelions in his waistband
A breeze scales his bare back and stirs
The tufts of grey hair on his shoulders
Each morning as the trees grow
Full and noisy with birds
She blinks her copper eyelids for the sun
Pointing to a plot of tulips
To kale that sat out winter in its coldframe
But she empties their home every morning
Today a crock pot tomorrow his fourposter
Today a record crate tomorrow her clawfoot
A candyfloss heap of pink fibreglass
Tomorrow support beams   strips of linoleum
Their windows will diamond the sidewalk

THERE WAS NOTHING LEFT TO DRINK

There was nothing left to drink,
and so we floated—fortified and aimless—
away from the party, down the emptying highway,
and you put your hand in your pocket, then mine
while we batted through Queen Anne's lace
to the water, where you unknotted
the rubber dinghy we found there,
and we both paused to see if it would puncture
when you placed your stiletto inside our inflatable boat.

YOU'D HAVE TO PAY ME COULD YOU PAY ME ENOUGH

You'd have to pay us
Could you pay us enough
To live for a stretch
Again in that house
Rippling through rooms
Papered with boys
Papered with dogs
As a means of escape imagining
Ourselves into every bad painting
Even ones of the purplest hell?
One of us moved
Through the house like a draft
She was tired
She said
She was empty
She was letting her body
Thin out and grow hairy
One day we brought
A picnic to her room
Spread it out like a stain
Waited for days
Checked our faces
In the tiny round mirrors embedded
In the skirt she'd left
We knew she'd abandoned
The house on a whim
(Like a blazer)
(Or a newborn)
We watched the apples soften

We watched the bread turn blue
We noted the second the sparkling
Water went still

THE LAST TIME I SLEPT IN THIS BED

I was involved in the serious business
of ripping apart my own body.

I'd run my fingers over it,
seeking but never finding

the right point of entry,
so having to tear one myself,

though midway through
I'd always tire,

and let night enter
like a silver needle,

sewing my eyelids shut.
This was not an original practice,

but thinking, for a time, that it *was*
felt like being able to choose

when spring would arrive:
engineering an April

that opened like a parasol,
even in thoroughest winter.

NOTES

The last four words of "Mary Ellen Spook" were supposedly the last words of Anneliese Michel, a German woman who was believed to be possessed by demons. She died in 1976 after undergoing sixty-seven "exorcism sessions."

The last ten lines of "The Sword Dance" are intended to recall Frank Bidart's poem "Tu Fu Watches the Spring Festival Across Serpentine Lake."

The title and first two lines of "Romance" are intended to recall Arthur Rimbaud's poem "Roman."

"Dead Boy Had Too Many Injuries To Fit In One Drawing" is about the murder of four-year-old Jérémy Bastien-Perron, in Montreal in 2008. "Dead Boy Had Too Many Injuries To Fit In One Drawing, Pathologist Says" is the full title of an article about the case, published in the *Montreal Gazette*.

ACKNOWLEDGMENTS

I am deeply grateful to the institutions that provided support, while I was writing this book: Boston University's Creative Writing Program, the Martha's Vineyard Writer's Residency, the Canada Council for the Arts, and Stanford University's Stegner Fellowship Program.

I am indebted to the editors of the magazines and journals in which some of these poems first appeared: *B O D Y*, *Maisonneuve*, *Poetry*, *Slate*, *The Threepenny Review*, *This Magazine*, and *The Walrus*.

To everyone at House of Anansi, but most especially Meredith Dees, Lynn Gammie, Sarah MacLachlan, Peter Norman, and Laura Repas.

To Brian Morgan, for his exquisite work designing this book.

I have had many brilliant, patient teachers. R.E.N. Allen, Eavan Boland, Stephanie Bolster, W.S. Di Piero, Ken Fields, Carla Funk, Louise Glück, David McGimpsey, Robert Pinsky, Derek Walcott, and Rosanna Warren. Among these, I would like to thank Robert Pinsky, in particular, for his incredible kindness, insight, and support.

To my friends, some of whom read this book in its early stages. Ann Bigelow, Adam Brown, Marjorie Celona, Larissa Diakiw, Erica Ehrenberg, Miriam Bird Greenberg, Speireag Hendra, Anastasia Jones, Antoinette Karuna, Emile Karuna, Emily Leithauser, Jessica Mensch, Julie Stinson, Max Smith, Lorraine Price, Katye Seip, Michelle Tompkins, Adam Tragakis, and Chris Tragakis. I love you.

To all my family, but especially Ta, my parents, Janis and Phonse, my brothers and sisters, Michael, Morgan, Nicholas, Marcus, Mariann, and Stephen, and my cousin Meghan. I love you.

To my editor, Jared Bland, in whom I am able to place perfect trust.

Sara Peters was born in Antigonish, Nova Scotia. She completed an MFA at Boston University, and was a Stegner Fellow in poetry at Stanford University from 2010 to 2012. Her poems have appeared in *Slate, Maisonneuve, This Magazine, B O D Y, The Threepenny Review, The Walrus,* and *Poetry.* She lives in Toronto.